DATE DUE

TRADITIONAL TALES

from

SOUTH AMERICA

Vic Parker

Based on myths and legends retold by
Philip Ardagh

Illustrated by
Syrah Arnold

Thameside Press

Distributed in the United States by
Smart Apple Media
1980 Lookout Drive
North Mankato, MN 56003

Text copyright © Vic Parker 2001

Editor: Stephanie Turnbull
Designer: Zoë Quayle
Educational consultant: Margaret Bellwood

Library of Congress Cataloging-in-Publication Data

Parker, Vic.
    South America / written by Vic Parker.
      p. cm. -- (Traditional tales from around the world)
    Includes index.
    Summary: A collection of tales from various South American Indian
cultures, including Caraja, Bororo, Tupinamba, Sherente, and others.
    ISBN 1-930643-40-3
    1. Indians of South America--Folklore. 2. Tales--South America. [1.
Indians of South America--Folklore. 2. Folklore--South America.] I. Title.

F2230.1.F6 P37 2001
398.2'098--dc21

                                    2001027185

Printed in Hong Kong

9 8 7 6 5 4 3 2 1

CONTENTS

SOUTH AMERICAN TALES

South America is enormous. It contains many separate countries. To the west stretches the longest mountain chain in the world, the Andes. To the south lie wide, grassy plains. Much of the rest of the land is covered by the largest jungle in the world, the Amazonian rainforest. It is named after the mighty Amazon river, which flows through it.

South America includes the countries of Brazil, Argentina, Peru, Chile, and Colombia. Today, most of the people in these countries live in big cities. Long, long ago, South Americans lived in groups in the mountains, plains, and jungle. These groups often shared spiritual beliefs, but they had different languages and different ways of life. Some were farmers, others were hunters or warriors.

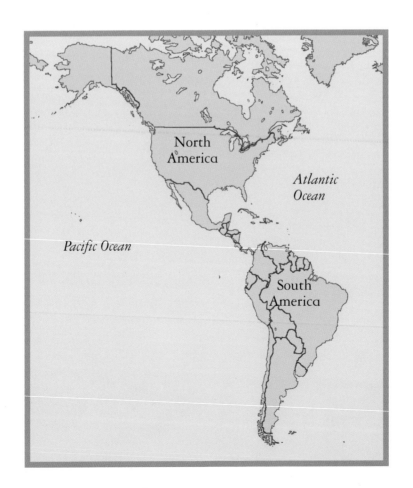

One group was the Inca tribe. They fought and conquered many other tribes and built a great empire. The Inca people worshiped the sun. They made many beautiful treasures from gold because it shone like the sun.

Around 500 years ago, white Europeans began arriving in South America. They killed many Incas or made them slaves, then they took the Incas' gold for themselves.

South American tribes believed that the world all around them was holy, and they worshiped certain mountains, rivers, plants, and animals. The tribes told many wonderful stories about spirits, gods, and magic. You can read new versions of some of these favorite old tales in this book.

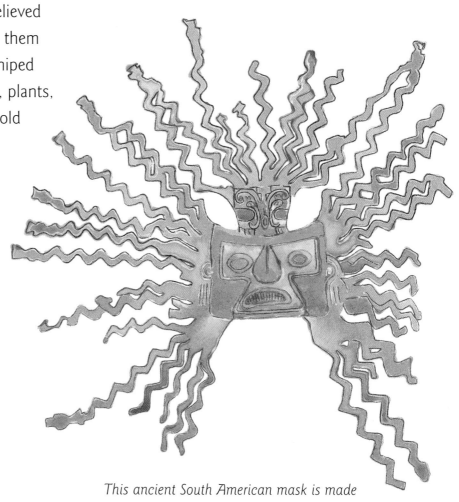

This ancient South American mask is made of gold and shaped to look like the sun.

A World of Endless Skies

The people of the Caraja tribe believe that long, long ago, humans did not live on the surface of the earth. They lived inside it. Every morning, the sun traveled down into the underground world from somewhere above the Earth. Every evening, the sun rose back out of the Earth.

No one knew where the sun went at night, for no one had ever followed it out of the Earth. One man was particularly curious about what lay above the surface. He was a wise man named Kaboi.

At night, Kaboi lay in bed and listened. If he kept very still and listened very carefully, he sometimes heard a strange cry coming through the layers of rock far above him. Kaboi had no idea who or what was making the noise, and it nearly drove him mad with wondering.

One night, the cry was louder and clearer than ever and Kaboi could stand it no longer. He woke his friends and explained, "I must know what that sound is! I think there must be another world above the Earth and the cry is coming from there. I am going to follow it and find out—even if it leads where no one has ever gone before."

7

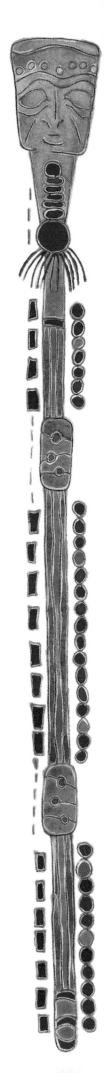

"That might be dangerous!" warned his friends.

"I know," said Kaboi, "but I am determined."

"Then we will go with you," declared his friends.

Tears sparkled in Kaboi's eyes at his friends' loyalty and bravery. The little band of men and women began to climb the rock walls of the underworld. Up . . . up . . . up . . . they clambered, high into the unknown. They climbed so high that they lost sight of the ground. They climbed so high that their arms and legs grew shaky with tiredness. They climbed so high that the strange cry seemed to be coming from just above their heads.

Suddenly the friends felt a strange sensation. Air was moving around them—it was wind. No one had ever felt wind before. They lifted their faces and enjoyed the coolness of the breeze blowing around them.

Next the friends smelled something sweet wafting toward them on the wind. They sniffed the wonderful scent. They did not know it, but it was the smell of grass.

Kaboi peered above him, and over his head was a hole in the rock that led into a long tunnel. The strange cry came floating down the tunnel, and Kaboi's friends cheered.

"It's true! There *is* another place up above!" they yelled.

Kaboi's heart thumped inside his chest as he reached up and pulled his head and shoulders into the tunnel.

8

He couldn't wait to see what lay on the other side....
But to Kaboi's great dismay, his tummy was too fat
to go through the hole! No matter how hard he pulled
and kicked and struggled, he simply couldn't squeeze
through. Kaboi wriggled back out again, panting.

"I cannot go," he sighed sadly. "My friends, you must
go for me. Explore this new world and tell me all about it."

Kaboi's friends hesitated. They were excited at the
thought of being the first people to go above the Earth's
surface, but they could see how disappointed Kaboi
was not to be able to go himself.

"Go," Kaboi urged. "Find out what makes the sound
that keeps me awake at night."

The men and women disappeared into the tunnel
and left Kaboi alone underground.

One by one, Kaboi's friends came out of the tunnel
and stood on the surface of the Earth. They could not
believe what they saw. Instead of a ceiling of rock above
them, there was endless air of the most beautiful color
they had ever seen. They were looking at the blue sky.
All around were trees, grass, and flowers colored like
bright jewels. Birds and butterflies soared and dipped
on the wind, and animals scampered all around.

"Kaboi has found paradise!" one man gasped.

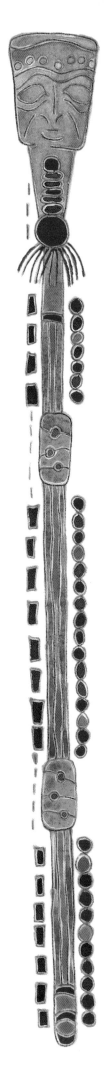

9

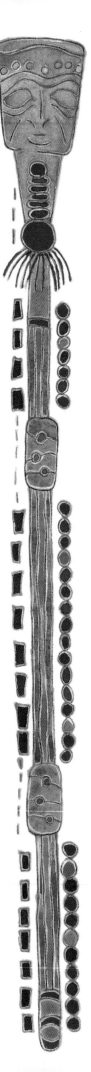

"Everyone will want to live here," exclaimed a woman.

Another of Kaboi's friends tried to speak, but his voice was drowned out by the loud, strange cry they had heard before. Everyone laughed with delight as they realized at last where it came from—a bird called a seriema.

"Let's hurry back to Kaboi and give him the answers he longed for!" cried the people. "Let's take things to show him, too." They gathered fruit, bees, honey, and a piece of dry wood from a dead tree. Then they climbed back into the tunnel and hurried down to the world below.

Kaboi wept tears of happiness when he saw his friends returning with shining eyes and beaming faces. He listened with joy as they told him about the creature that made the strange cry and all the other wonderful sights in the world above. He inspected the things his friends had brought back with them, and he marveled at them all.

First, Kaboi sniffed the fruit and bit into it nervously. How good it tasted!

"What a wonderful world it must be, to produce such delicious food," he declared.

Next, Kaboi studied the bees and the honeycomb.

"The creatures of the upper world work hard," he said wisely, "and the result of their work is very sweet!"

Finally, Kaboi examined the dead wood. He frowned.

"Where did this come from?" he asked in a serious, stern voice.

"I found it on a tree," one man explained.

"Are all trees made of this?" said Kaboi in a low voice.

"No," admitted the man. "The other trees were green and straight and tall. This one was lying down and had no leaves at all."

Kaboi shook his head sadly. "This new world is certainly beautiful, but it is a world where things grow old and die. This wood is from a tree that is no longer alive and growing. I fear that if we go to live in this world, we will one day wither away and die, too."

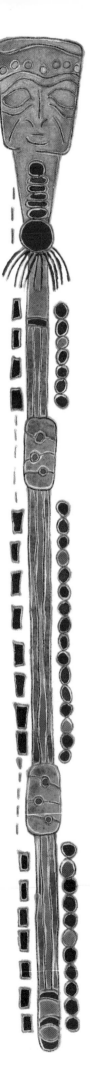

Kaboi's friends were shocked and silent. They found it hard to understand what he was saying. They had never thought of becoming wrinkled and weak—and then suddenly not being anything at all. But their eyes still shone with the beauty of the world up above. Their hearts were still full of the new sights and sounds they had enjoyed. They decided that the price of death was worth paying to be able to live in such a wonderful place.

With a heavy heart, the wise Kaboi decided to stay underground. Here he lived a peaceful but lonely life forevermore. His friends went to live short but joyful lives in the land above the Earth. We are all descended from these people, so that's how we came to live in this beautiful world of endless skies—and that's why we all grow old and die.

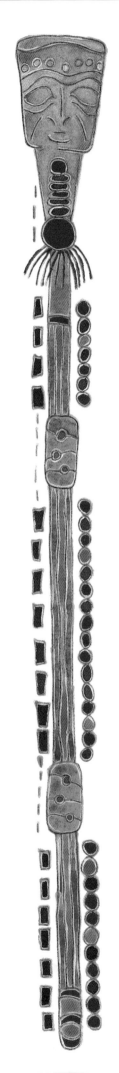

How the
Stars Came

As usual, the hot morning sun was shining on the village of the Bororo tribe. As usual, the men were away hunting in the thick, green forest. As usual, the women had gone to the maize fields to collect cobs of corn. As usual, one little boy was left behind with his grandmother.

The little one wished he could go to the maize fields because he was very good at finding corn cobs. He was so small that he could duck underneath the tall, waving stalks and find the corn cobs that had fallen on the ground. All the same, the little one didn't really mind staying with his grandmother. She had a pet macaw, a brightly colored bird that could talk. The little one loved to help his grandmother teach the bird new words.

This particular morning, however, the women came hurrying back to the village after only an hour or two. Their baskets were empty and their faces were worried.

"Little one," they pleaded, "we can find no corn cobs today. Come with us and help us if you can."

The little one grinned and ran to the fields. Sure enough, he found corn cob after corn cob after corn cob.

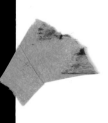

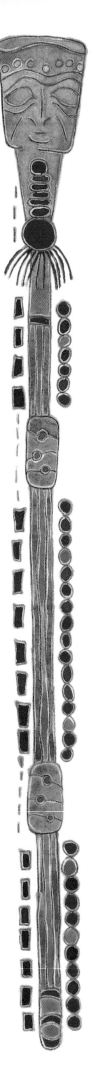

Before long the women's baskets were nearly full. Chatting and singing happily, they sat under some shady trees and stripped the sweetcorn from the cobs. Next they pounded the sweetcorn on flat stones until it was a fine flour. Later they would make tasty pancakes for everyone's supper. How pleased their husbands would be when they returned from hunting!

As the little one watched the women, he grew jealous. *I found the corn cobs!* he thought to himself. *That flour is really mine. Most of the pancakes should be for me and my friends!*

The women were so busy working and talking that they didn't notice the little one slipping among them. Time and time again, the little one scooped up a handful of flour when no one was looking. He scampered away with it and hid it in the hollow middle of a bamboo shoot. Before long, the little one had filled so many bamboo shoots that he had enough flour for a feast!

The little one had a greedy gleam in his eye as he hurried back to the village, smiling secretly to himself.

"Grandma, look!" the little one laughed, as he emptied the bamboo shoots and the flour spilled out. "Will you cook this into pancakes for me and my friends?"

His grandmother's eyes opened wide with surprise.

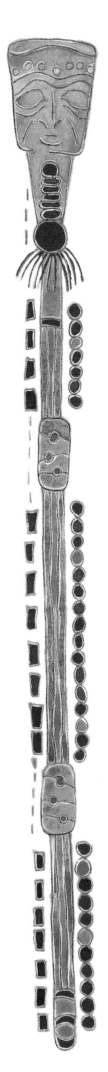

"Wherever did you get all that flour from, little one?" she gasped.

"LITTLE ONE!" squawked the macaw, echoing her words.

"You didn't steal it, did you?" asked Grandma sternly.

"Of course not!" lied the boy. "I found so many corn cobs that the women had more than enough flour. They said that I could take as much as I could carry"

"CARRY!" screeched the macaw, learning a new word.

Grandma frowned. She didn't know whether to believe her mischievous grandson or not.

"Pleeeeease, Grandma," the little one begged, looking up at his grandmother very sweetly.

"Oh, very well then," she smiled.

At once, the delighted little one sneaked around the village, inviting all his friends to his feast. Meanwhile, his grandmother measured and poured and mixed and fried. Delicious smells wafted up from her stove.

This really is an awful lot of flour, she thought to herself, as worries crept back into her mind. *Surely the women didn't allow the little one to have all this.*

Grandma's fears deepened as she watched the children tuck into the pancakes. They whispered and giggled together as if they were sharing a naughty secret.

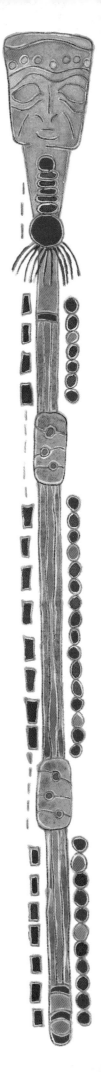

"Is my little one a thief?" Grandma muttered to herself.

"THIEF!" shrieked the macaw. "THIEF! THIEF!"

The shocked children fell silent.

That bird has found out that I stole the flour! thought the little one. *It will give me away!*

In a panic, the little one snatched the bird and cut out its tongue. Some people say that he was instantly very sorry. Other people say that he didn't care a bit and cut out his grandmother's tongue, too. Whatever the case, the bad deed was done—and as you know, wickedness is as catching as a cold. The children ran away, stolen flour and crumbs still around their mouths. Giggling, they opened all the cages of all the birds in the village, letting every single pet escape.

The little one sat down with his head in his hands. "This is all my fault!" he moaned. "When the grown-ups come back and discover what we've done, they'll punish us all!"

The children decided there was only one thing to do. They had to escape to where the grown-ups wouldn't find them. They knew that grown-ups weren't very good climbers because they were too heavy, so the children decided to hide high in the sky.

The first thing they did was to find a long creeper.

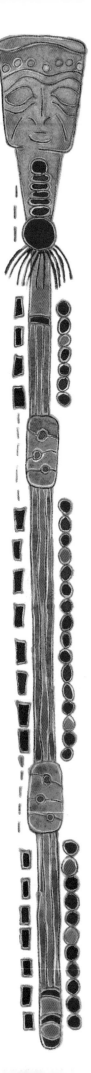

Next they asked a hummingbird to fly with one end of the creeper into the sky and tie it fast. Finally, one by one, the children scrambled up the creeper and into the heavens.

Meanwhile, the women had left the maize fields and were on their way home. As soon as they drew near, they knew that something was wrong. They couldn't hear the usual happy sounds of the children laughing and playing. Instead, the whole village was silent except for the little one's grandmother wailing over her poor macaw.

The horrified women dropped their baskets and ran frantically in and out of the houses. All their children were gone! Suddenly they noticed the legs of the very last child climbing up the creeper into the clouds. Quickly, the desperate women ran to the creeper and began to heave themselves up.

The children were right. The grown-ups were too heavy to follow them. The creeper snapped with an ear-splitting CRACK, and the children's mothers, aunts, sisters, and cousins went tumbling and screaming through the air.

Fortunately, the Earth took pity on the poor women who had tried to follow their loved ones.

The women weren't killed when they hit the dust. Instead they were turned into all kinds of animals that scampered and slithered and hopped away.

When the men of the village returned home from hunting that evening, they found that all the women and all the children had mysteriously disappeared. Even more mysteriously, there were strange lights twinkling in the night sky that had not been there before.

Today we know these lights as stars. The children are still trapped in the heavens, where they never grow old. The stars are their eyes, twinkling with tears as they weep for the bad things they did.

EARTH, FIRE, AND FLOOD

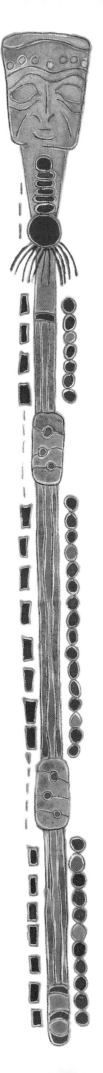

According to the Tupinamba people, at the beginning of time the Earth had no mountains, hills, or valleys. All the land was completely flat. There weren't even any seas, just lakes of fresh water.

This world was made and cared for by a very powerful god called Monan, who lived in Heaven. Monan created people too and these humans praised and worshiped him. This made Monan very happy, and he let his humans do whatever they liked. Monan thought of people as if they were spoiled children. He found it amusing to watch his humans carrying on in their odd little ways, getting up to all sorts of mischief.

As time went by, people became ungrateful.

"We don't need Monan," they began to say to each other. "We have all we need without him."

They took it for granted that the sun would rise every morning and set every evening. They forgot that Monan was in charge of it all.

"Yes, what does Monan do for us?" others asked.

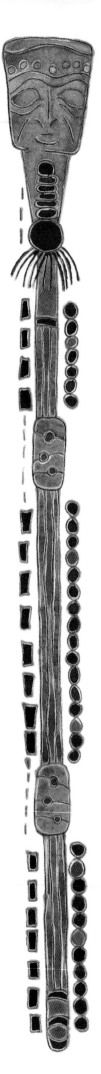

They forgot that he made fruit and crops grow for them. They ignored the fact that Monan filled the Earth with animals and birds and fish.

All over the world, humans began to criticize Monan.

"Monan has made summer too hot," some grumbled.

"Monan has made water too wet," moaned others.

"Monan has made trees too tall and fruit too sweet," whined more men and women.

Worst of all, many humans stopped believing that Monan existed at all! They gave up thinking about him and praying to him. They laughed and joked when people spoke his name. Others simply forgot about Monan altogether.

Nobody likes to have no friends, so you can imagine how upset the poor god felt. For a while, Monan kept hoping that people would see how silly they were being and turn back to him. Finally he realized that this wasn't going to happen, and then he became very angry.

"These stupid, rude, ungrateful humans must be punished!" he roared. "They do not deserve to live in the beautiful world I have created especially for them!"

The great god sent down a blazing fire from Heaven to destroy everyone on Earth—but, just in time, he scooped up one man into the safety of his hand.

To tell the truth, deep down the creator god was still fond of his humans, and he couldn't bear to see all of them wiped out forever.

Monan's fire was so fierce that it not only burned all the people and creatures to a cinder, but it also made the Earth itself melt and bend into folds and creases. This is how the world came to have mountains and hills and valleys.

The man that Monan had saved looked down from Heaven and saw the raging flames leaping higher and higher all over the Earth. He was very scared indeed.

"Great creator!" he cried respectfully. "If you do not stop the blaze, your flames will eat up the skies and stars too! You will destroy your own home!"

Monan sighed. The man was right. He was getting carried away. In the twinkling of an eye, Monan made it rain. It rained like it has never rained before or since. Waterfalls came pouring out of the heavens as if Monan had turned on gigantic faucets in the skies. The rain washed over the surface of the whole world in a huge flood, putting out the fire at once. The land fizzed and hissed and sizzled as the waters cooled the ashes and swirled them into enormous, salty oceans—which still cover much of the Earth to this day.

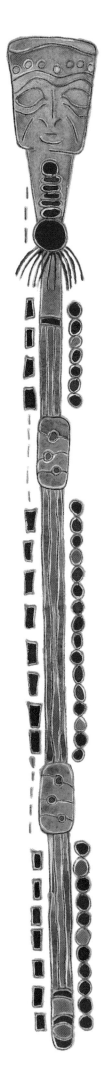

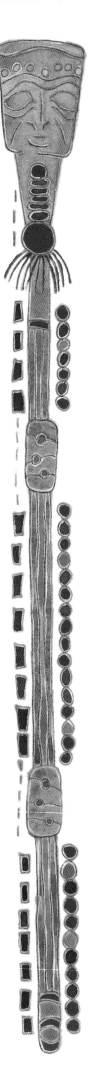

Monan looked down and thought that the world seemed to be washed clean. He liked the way it looked now that it was all bumpy with mountains. He admired the way the salty seas sparkled in the light of the sun. He peered at the nervous man in his hand.

"You don't belong with me in the heavens," Monan said. "You belong on Earth." Gently, Monan put the man on the ground.

"Thank you, great creator," said the man, bowing low. "You saved my life and now you are returning me to your beautiful world. I will never forget your kindness."

Monan was delighted. "You are a good man!" he cried. "I do not want you to be lonely down there on your own. I will create a companion for you, and you can both enjoy my world together." Monan made a wife for the man and placed her on Earth with him.

The man and woman lived happily together and in time had many children who went to live all over the Earth. The man and woman named one boy baby Maira-Monan after the creator god himself. This son grew into a powerful holy man, or shaman.

Maira-Monan was a wise man, and he learned many secrets of nature, such as how to make fire and how to grow crops. His magic was truly mighty.

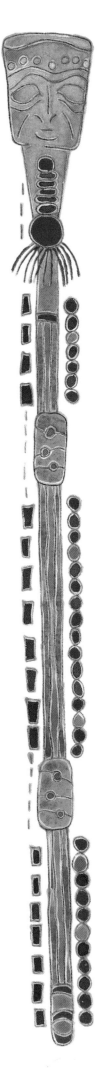

After the flood, the creator god had stocked the Earth with many kinds of trees and plants, but all the animals he made looked the same! Maira-Monan worked magic to make them all wonderfully different. Maira-Monan filled the waters with sharks and crabs and sea horses and dolphins and other sea creatures. He filled the land with monkeys and armadillos and tortoises and lizards and other animals. He filled the air with parrots and bees and eagles and dragonflies and other birds and insects.

Maira-Monan was so powerful that other people became afraid of him.

"Maira-Monan might turn on us one day like the creator god did," they murmured fearfully to each other. "He might try to wipe us all out! We must stop him!"

One day, the people asked Maira-Monan to come to a certain village to display his powers. The great shaman liked the idea of showing off his magic, so he agreed. Little did he know that the people had come up with a wicked plot to trap him!

The cunning humans asked Maira-Monan to walk through a magic fire and use his great skills to come out unharmed. The fire didn't singe so much as a hair on his head. The humans then asked Maira-Monan to walk through a second fire.

This fire contained rare and powerful magic, but Maira-Monan walked straight into it, not thinking that it would be any more dangerous than the last.

As soon as Maira-Monan stepped into the flames, he disappeared in an explosion of bright light followed by a deafening noise that seemed to tear the sky in two.

To this very day, the gods still send us lightning and thunder in memory of the great Maira-Monan. It also reminds us of the time when the creator god sent the biggest storm the world has ever seen and gave humans a second chance on Earth.

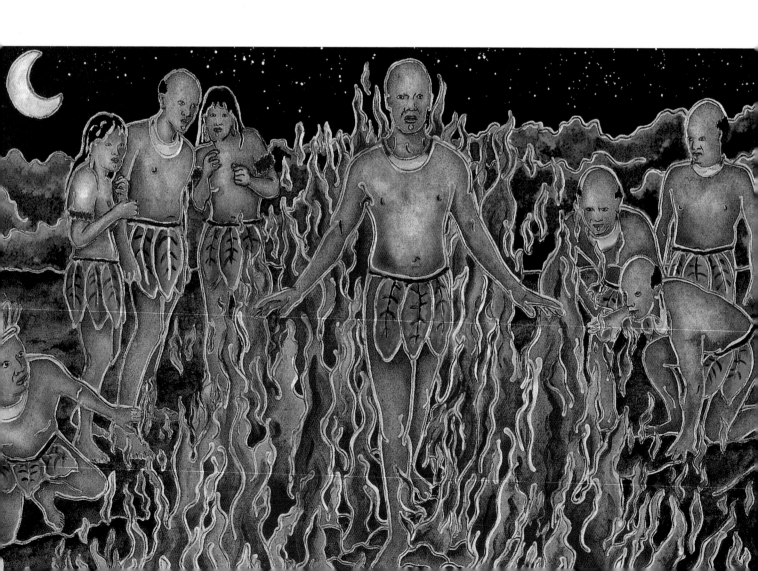

Asare and the Alligators

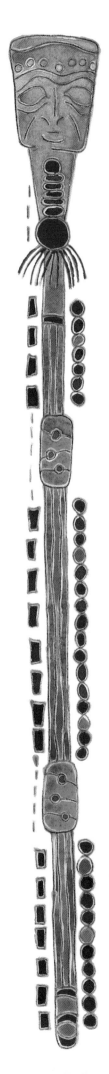

There is an old Sherente tale that tells of seven brothers who were cast out of their village as a punishment for making trouble. The brothers had nowhere to live, and so they went wandering through the rainforest.

"What will happen if we meet a snake?" one of the brothers said nervously. The rainforest was a wild, deep jungle as high as the sky and as wide as the sunrise. It was full of all sorts of sharp-toothed beasts, poisonous frogs, flesh-eating fish and other fierce creatures.

"What will we eat?" another brother asked worriedly. The youngest brother, Asare, had a lucky arrow with which he had hunted a few small lizards—but this was hardly going to be enough for seven starving brothers!

"Where can we find something to drink?" gasped Asare. After walking for hours with no sign of water, his throat was as dry as the dust that hung in the sunlight.

"I know the answer to that one," said the eldest brother. "Look over there." He pointed to a cluster of tucum nuts dangling from a tree. He knew that tucum nuts contained a sweet liquid that was refreshing to drink.

27

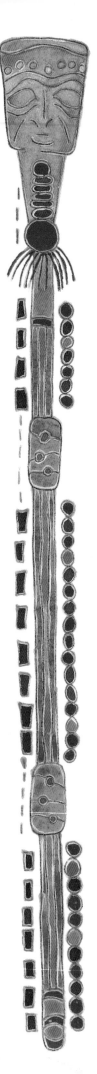

The weary brothers cheered up a little. They found a long stick and knocked the tucum nuts out of the tree. The brothers smashed open the shells and began to drink the tasty juice.

Glug . . . glug . . . glug.... Asare drank the liquid from nut after nut after nut—but he was still thirsty.

Then the sharp-eyed eldest brother saw a dark patch of soil. "If I'm not much mistaken," he grinned, "there might just be a spring under the ground over there."

"Let's start digging!" croaked the desperate Asare, and the excited brothers hurried to the spot. They scrabbled frantically in the dirt, first scooping with their hands and then with sharp sticks. Deeper and deeper and deeper they dug, and then—WHOOSH! A huge fountain of water burst out of the ground and gushed into the air. Asare drank and drank until he was fit to burst.

Meanwhile the water spurted into a stream, which poured into a river, which flowed away into the first lake, which turned into the first ocean.

At first the brothers were stunned by the gushing river that had formed next to them, but they soon started to laugh. "You won't go thirsty again, Asare!" they chuckled.

"No," said Asare, "but we might all go hungry! The river has washed away the lizards that I hunted!"

The brothers' faces fell. After their bit of luck they now felt just as downhearted as before.

"Never mind," Asare continued. "Do you want the good news or the bad news?"

"You mean there's *more* bad news?" one of the brothers groaned. "Well, let's have the good news first."

"The good news is that my lucky arrow hasn't been washed away," said Asare, beaming, "so I can catch some more lizards for our supper."

"What's the bad news?" asked the brothers nervously.

"The bad news is that my lucky arrow is now on the other side of that raging river," continued Asare. "But don't worry. I'll soon get it."

Before the brothers could stop him, the brave boy plunged into the rushing waters.

"Asare, you've forgotten something!" his brothers yelled desperately. "You can't swim!" They watched as Asare was carried away by the current and swept out of sight.

As Asare choked and spluttered and began to disappear under the water, his grasping fingers tightened around a floating log. But the floating log wasn't a floating log. It was an alligator that just looked a lot like a floating log. Asare didn't know what an alligator looked like because there had never been alligators on Earth before.

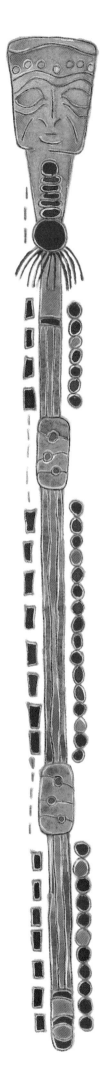

They had been created from Asare's lizards when the magic river washed them away.

"Let me sit on your back, Mister Ugly Long Nose," said Asare to the alligator.

"I'll give you *Mister Ugly Long Nose!*" sneered the alligator and he opened his razor-sharp jaws and snapped them at Asare.

Suddenly Asare found that he knew how to swim after all. He rocketed through the water and shot out onto the bank. He didn't stop once he was on dry land, but kept on running as fast as he could into the forest. Unfortunately, Asare didn't realize that alligators could run, too. Mister Ugly Long Nose was speeding along on his short, stubby legs and grinning a toothy grin very close to Asare's bottom!

Asare crashed into the undergrowth and heard the TAP-TAP of woodpeckers above him. He begged the busy birds for their help. To his relief, they showered him with pieces of bark until his body and his smell were both hidden. Asare looked just like a strange, scaly monster.

Mr Ugly Long Nose burst into view a moment later.

"Which way did he go?" panted the alligator.

"Who?" asked Asare innocently.

"That tasty human," snapped Mister Ugly Long Nose.

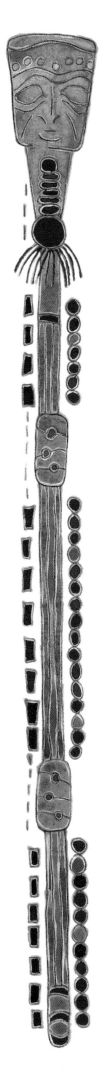

"He went that way!" said Asare, pointing deeper into the forest, and the alligator sprinted away while woodpecker laughter filled the air.

Asare thanked the clever birds, brushed off his disguise and dashed away in the opposite direction— only to come face to face with another alligator!

"HELP!" Asare yelled as he ran into the undergrowth again. This time he headed in the direction of some chattering, giggling monkeys.

The monkeys thought that Asare was an extremely funny sight, all muddy from the river, red from running, and covered in sticky bits of bark like scales. They laughed so hard that they nearly fell out of their trees.

"Quick! Please help me! Tell me what to do!" begged Asare.

The monkeys were chuckling too much to speak. They held their sides and pointed to a huge pile of skins left over from the jatoba fruit they were eating.

Asare jumped underneath the skins a split second before the alligator found the monkeys, too.

"Have you seen a tasty human?" asked the alligator, licking his lips.

"Ha-ha-ha!" laughed the monkeys.

"Have you seen a tasty human?" drooled the alligator.

"Hee-hee-hee!" chortled the monkeys.

"I said—oh, forget it!" grunted the alligator. He knew he wouldn't get any sense out of the silly creatures, so he gave up and stomped away. Asare crawled out of the pile of fruit skins and thanked the monkeys for their help.

Asare lived to have many other adventures, or so the Sherente people say. Like all good stories, his has a happy ending. At long last, Asare caught up with his brothers, who were delighted to find him alive. After bathing in the new ocean, they were all so clean and shiny that they now gleam in the sky as stars—known to this day as the Seven Brothers.

FIRE AND THE JAGUAR

Long, long ago, humans didn't know how to make fire. When darkness fell, people had no light. When the weather grew cold, people shivered. When people tracked down animals for food, they dried the meat in the sun and ate it raw. How did humans come to know the secret of fire? The Kayapo tribes believe they know, although there are several versions of the story....

A man and a boy called Botoque were out hunting one day, when the man spied a macaw's nest on a ledge at the top of some tall rocks.

"Climb up there and see if there are any eggs, Botoque!" the man ordered.

"Do I have to?" sighed Botoque, peering up at the towering ledge.

"Yes!" commanded the man—so that was that.

Botoque was small and light-footed, but the rock face was steep and there were no handholds or footholds. Each time Botoque tried to climb, he came sliding back down with scraped knees and hands. After a while he stopped, exhausted. It was impossible to climb the rocks.

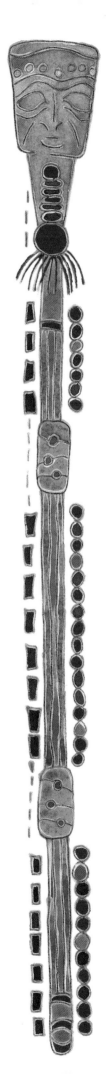

35

"You give up too easily!" sneered the man. He stalked off into the thick undergrowth. After a few minutes, he staggered back, dragging a fallen tree trunk. He took an ax from his belt and chopped some footholds into the wood. "There you are, Botoque," he smirked. "A ladder."

Heaving and panting, he and Botoque hauled the tree trunk up straight and leaned it against the rocks. It was a very tall trunk, but it only just reached the ledge where the nest was perched. It looked as if it was a long way up.

"Please hold the ladder steady," Botoque said nervously.

"Of course," replied the man. "Now get going!"

Botoque gulped and began to climb.

Up . . . up . . . up.... Botoque clung to the long, thin ladder. The higher he climbed, the more the tree trunk bounced under him. He gripped it tightly with his fingers and toes.

At last Botoque reached the top of the tree trunk and stepped onto the rocky ledge. He didn't dare look down.

"How many eggs are there?" shouted the man.

Botoque peered into the nest. He couldn't believe his eyes. There were no eggs at all, just two round stones. He picked them up and yelled back, "There aren't any eggs!"

The man squinted into the sunlight. "Then what are you holding in your hands?" he bellowed.

"These are just stones," Botoque yelled back. "Now hold the ladder steady— I'm coming down!"

As Botoque put one foot onto the tree trunk, the man roared with rage. "I don't believe you! I think you're lying! Those are tasty eggs and you want them for yourself!" He began to shake the bottom of the ladder in anger.

"Stop!" Botoque yelled in panic, as he swayed this way and that. "I'm not lying!"

He made a grab for the rocky ledge with both hands and jumped back onto it but, in doing so, he dropped the two stones. WHEEE! Down they fell through the air. CRACK! SMACK! They landed right on the man below. Shocked, the man let go of the tree trunk, and it fell to the ground with an almighty crash. The man was so furious that he didn't care about Botoque, stuck on the rocky ledge. He just strode off through the forest, ignoring Botoque's cries for help.

Poor Botoque clung to the rocky ledge for several days and nights. No one from his village came to find him because the wicked man had told everybody that Botoque had been naughty and run away. Botoque was all alone. He was worn out and very hungry and thirsty. He grew so thin that he didn't look human anymore, but like a strange bag of skin and bones.

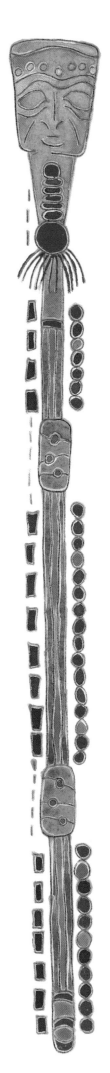

At last a big, wild cat called a jaguar came prowling over the rocks. His paws stuck to the steep rock face like glue.

"What kind of creature are you?" he asked, sniffing curiously at Botoque.

"I'm a human," wheezed Botoque hoarsely.

"I didn't think that humans lived on rocky ledges," said the jaguar.

"We don't," croaked Botoque. "I can't get down."

"Let me help you," replied the kind jaguar. "I will take you home and look after you like my own son."

Botoque gratefully climbed on the big cat's back and the jaguar leaped down the rocks and off into the jungle.

In the jaguar's house a few logs lay on the floor, glowing with light. Bright, moving colors of red, orange, and yellow sprang from them. When Botoque came near them, he felt hotter. Botoque was amazed.

"Is that a kind of magic?" he gasped.

"It's fire," the jaguar explained. "We cook with it."

Botoque watched the jaguar's wife roast some meat on the fire, then they ate it for supper. Botoque thought it was delicious—much better than the raw meat he was used to eating. And that is how Botoque became the first of his people—perhaps the first of all humans— to see a fire and eat meat cooked on one.

Next morning, the jaguar took Botoque hunting with him. The jaguar didn't use his teeth and claws to hunt— he had a bow and arrow. Botoque was amazed. He had never seen a bow and arrow before, because humans did not know about such things.

Day after day, the jaguar showed Botoque many new things, and they became close friends. The jaguar's wife, on the other hand, didn't like Botoque at all. When the two were alone, the jaguar's wife snarled fiercely at Botoque and swiped at him with her razor-sharp claws.

One morning, when the jaguar was out hunting by himself, the jaguar's wife pounced furiously at Botoque. Quick as a flash, Botoque snatched up his bow. He fired an arrow into her paw to defend himself, then he grabbed some cooked meat and ran for his life.

Botoque ran until he reached the safety of his own village. Everyone was stunned to see him alive and well. They were even more amazed to hear his stories about the clever jaguar. Botoque gave them each a bite of the cooked meat, and they agreed it was the most mouth-watering food they had ever tasted.

"We must have some of this fire for ourselves, so we can cook meat too," they decided.

That night, the villagers crept into the jaguar's house.

39

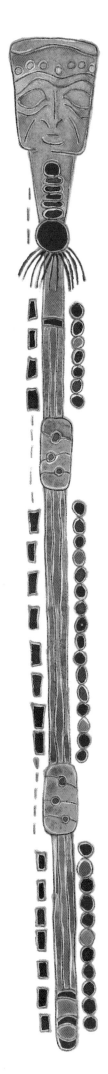

They stole a burning log and carried it away on the back of an animal called a tapir.

The villagers didn't think that the jaguar would notice that one burning log was gone. But the jaguar had been watching in the darkness. His heart was heavy with sadness. He had helped and loved Botoque, and now Botoque had betrayed him. The jaguar decided that he did not need fire anymore. There was fire now inside his heart—a flaming rage against humans. The jaguar swore that from that moment on he would never cook meat again, but eat all flesh raw. He would not hunt with a bow and arrow, but tear at his prey with his teeth and claws. And jaguars and humans have been enemies ever since....

THE STORY OF THE INCAS

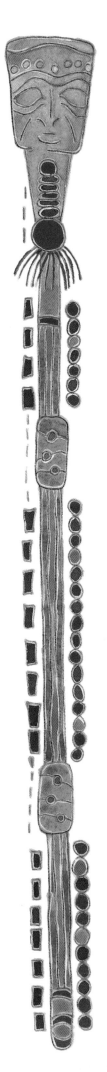

Long, long ago in South America, there was a place where three caves stood side by side. One day, four brothers and four sisters stepped out of the middle cave. They were strong and elegant and brave. Each was dressed in clothes of the finest, brightest material, and each carried treasures of precious, shining gold.

The four brothers were called "Ayar": Ayar Manco, Ayar Cachi, Ayar Auca, and Ayar Uchu. The four sisters were called "Mama": Mama Ocllo, Mama Raua, Mama Huaco, and Mama Cora.

Out of the caves on either side followed a whole race of men and women.

"These are the Incas, the chosen people of the sun," announced the eldest brother, Ayar Manco, to his brothers and sisters. "We must be their leaders. We must guide these men and women to a land where they can live happily and become a great nation."

Ayar Manco struck his golden staff on the ground. The soil was dry and hard, and the staff bounced off the ground with a dull thud.

41

"We will settle in the place where my staff sinks softly into the soil," Ayar Manco declared. The brothers and sisters then led the people away on their travels to find a homeland.

The Incas journeyed for many, many years. As time passed, one of the four brothers became more and more big-headed and boastful. Ayar Cachi loved to talk about how clever he was, and he never missed an opportunity to show off his magical powers. The other brothers and sisters grew tired of Ayar Cachi's reckless tricks, but Ayar Cachi never listened when they told him to stop.

One day, the brothers and sisters climbed to the top of a huge mountain. They gasped in delight as they looked down on the land spread out below them like a flat, colorful blanket.

"Now I know that we have found the place we will call home," declared Ayar Manco.

"How beautiful it is!" smiled the eldest sister, Mama Ocllo.

"Hmm . . . but I could improve it!" laughed Ayar Cachi.

Before his brothers and sisters could stop him, he grabbed some loose stones, slipped them into a slingshot, and began firing them at the ground below.

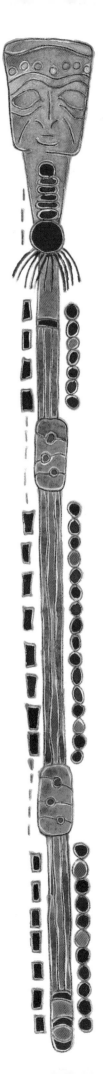

43

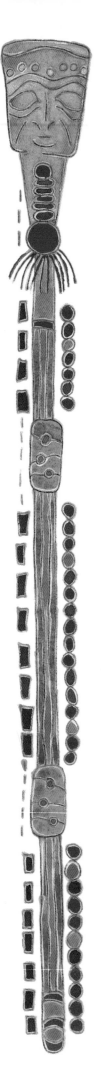

Ayar Cachi was so amazingly strong that the stones made huge valleys and enormous hills and gigantic gorges wherever they landed.

"See? I'm so powerful I can change the Earth itself!" Ayar Cachi cried gleefully.

The brothers and sisters looked at the proud Ayar Cachi in dismay. That night, they secretly discussed what they should do about their boastful brother.

"Ayar Cachi is becoming too powerful for his own good," worried Mama Ocllo.

"His magic strength has gone to his head, and he has lost all common sense," worried Ayar Uchu.

"Ayar Cachi may turn his strength against our people," said Mama Raua. "We cannot let that happen. We must protect the Incas, the chosen people of the sun."

"I think I know a way to stop Ayar Cachi," whispered Ayar Manco. The others crowded around as Ayar Manco explained what had to be done....

Next morning, the three brothers and four sisters went to Ayar Cachi and asked him to go on a very important mission.

"We want you to return to the cave we came from and fetch the sacred llama," they told their brother. A llama looks like a mixture of a horse and a sheep.

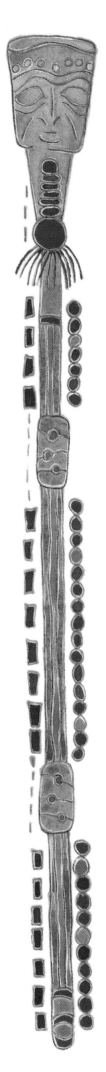

"We need the sacred llama to help us on our journey," they explained.

"Why do *I* have to go?" grumbled Ayar Cachi sulkily.

"Because you're the cleverest," said Mama Huaco.

Ayar Cachi's face brightened a little.

"Because you're the fastest," said Ayar Auca.

Ayar Cachi gave a little smile.

"Because you're the strongest," said Mama Cora.

Ayar Cachi beamed with pleasure. "Yes, I see now why I am the best person for the job," he agreed. "Very well. I will go." He started back to the cave at once.

Ayar Cachi was so carried away with the importance of his mission that he never stopped to think that it might be a trap. He never realized that his brothers and sisters were following him. As soon as Ayar Cachi had stepped into the middle cave, the brothers and sisters used their magic to seal it up behind him with a spell that even he could not break.

The three remaining brothers and their four sisters returned to the mountain where the Inca people were waiting for them. They prepared to set off for the wonderful land where they were going to settle, but just before they left, Ayar Uchu had an important announcement to make.

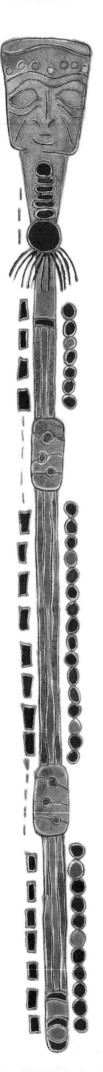

"I am going to stay in this high place," he declared calmly. "From here I can look down on the Incas' homeland and watch over our people."

As the last words passed Ayar Uchu's lips he turned to stone, so he could stay there forever. The grateful Incas built a shrine around the stone, and it became a holy place from that moment on.

Now there were two brothers left . . . but not for long. Ayar Auca soon decided that it was time for him to take his own path and travel alone. He said goodbye to his beloved family and people and went his own way. There are many tales that tell of Ayar Auca's great adventures before he too finally settled outside a city, guarding it forever as a sacred stone.

Ayar Manco was the only brother with the four sisters when they arrived at the homeland for the Incas, the chosen people of the sun. Just as he had said, Ayar Manco hit his golden staff on the ground and it sank into the soil—so far that it vanished out of sight.

"This is the place where our people will live happily," he announced.

After that, Ayar Manco was known as Manco Capac, the founder of the Inca kingdom. He and his sisters led wars against the people already living in the valley.

Through courage, wit, and strength, they eventually won the land for the Incas. Tales tell that Manco Capac and his four sisters even built the first houses there with their own hands.

Eventually, Manco Capac knew his work was done. He turned into a holy stone like his brothers, and his son took over as the leader of the Inca people. As for the Incas themselves, they became one of the world's great civilizations. The pyramid-shaped temples they built still stand today, thousands of years later.

INDEX